Sean Kenney

Cool City

Christy Ottaviano Books
Henry Holt and Company
New York

For Audrey

Henry Holt and Company, LLC
Publishers since 1866
175 Fifth Avenue
New York, New York 10010
mackids.com

Library of Congress Cataloging-in-Publication Data
Kenney, Sean.
Cool city / Sean Kenney. — 1st ed.
p. cm.
"Christy Ottaviano books."
ISBN 978-0-8050-8762-8
1. Miniature cities and towns—Juvenile literature.
2. Architectural models—Juvenile literature.
3. LEGO toys—Juvenile literature. I. Title.
TT178.K44 2011 745.5928—dc22 2010049001

First Edition—2011 / Book design by Elynn Cohen
LEGO bricks were used to create the models for this book.
The models were photographed by John E. Barrett.
Printed in the United States of America by Worzalla,
Stevens Point, Wisconsin

10 9 8 7 6 5 4

Let's build a city!

The city is a great place to be!

好好吃
Chinese Food

There are lots of things to see and to do . . .

1

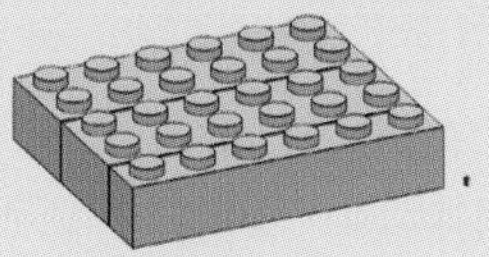

2

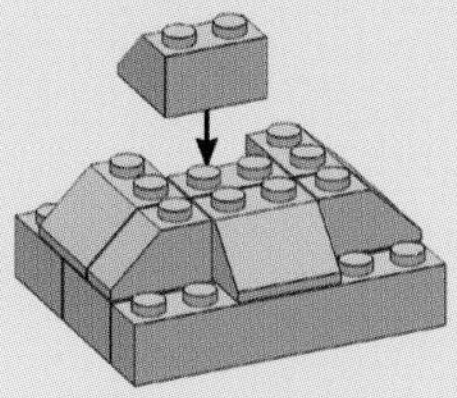

3

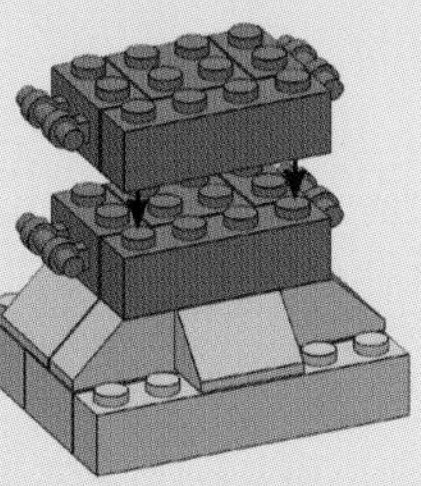

4

1

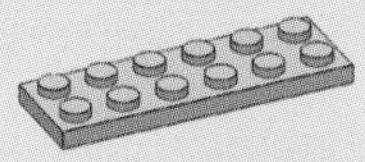

2

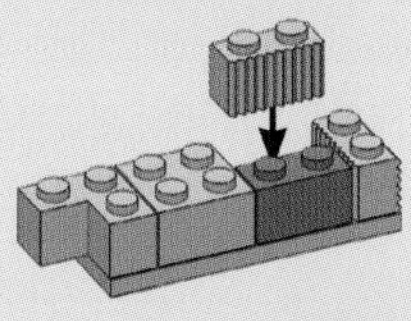

3

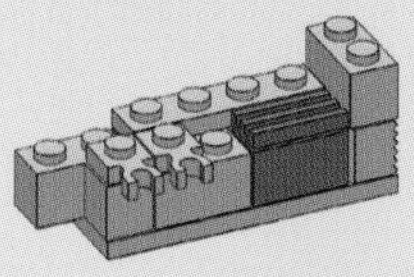

4

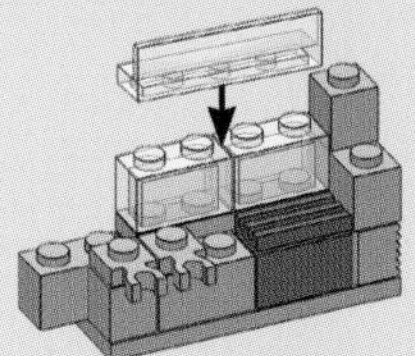

5

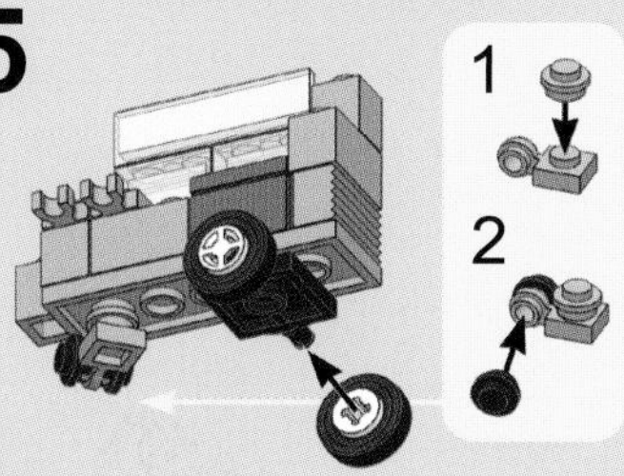

6

. . . whether you're underground . . .

X15 Main Street
Subway
Subway
Street
Entrance
Station
Ticket machines
Turnstiles
Platform
Pipes and gizmos

. . . or way up high.

Add gargoyles and other cool decorations.

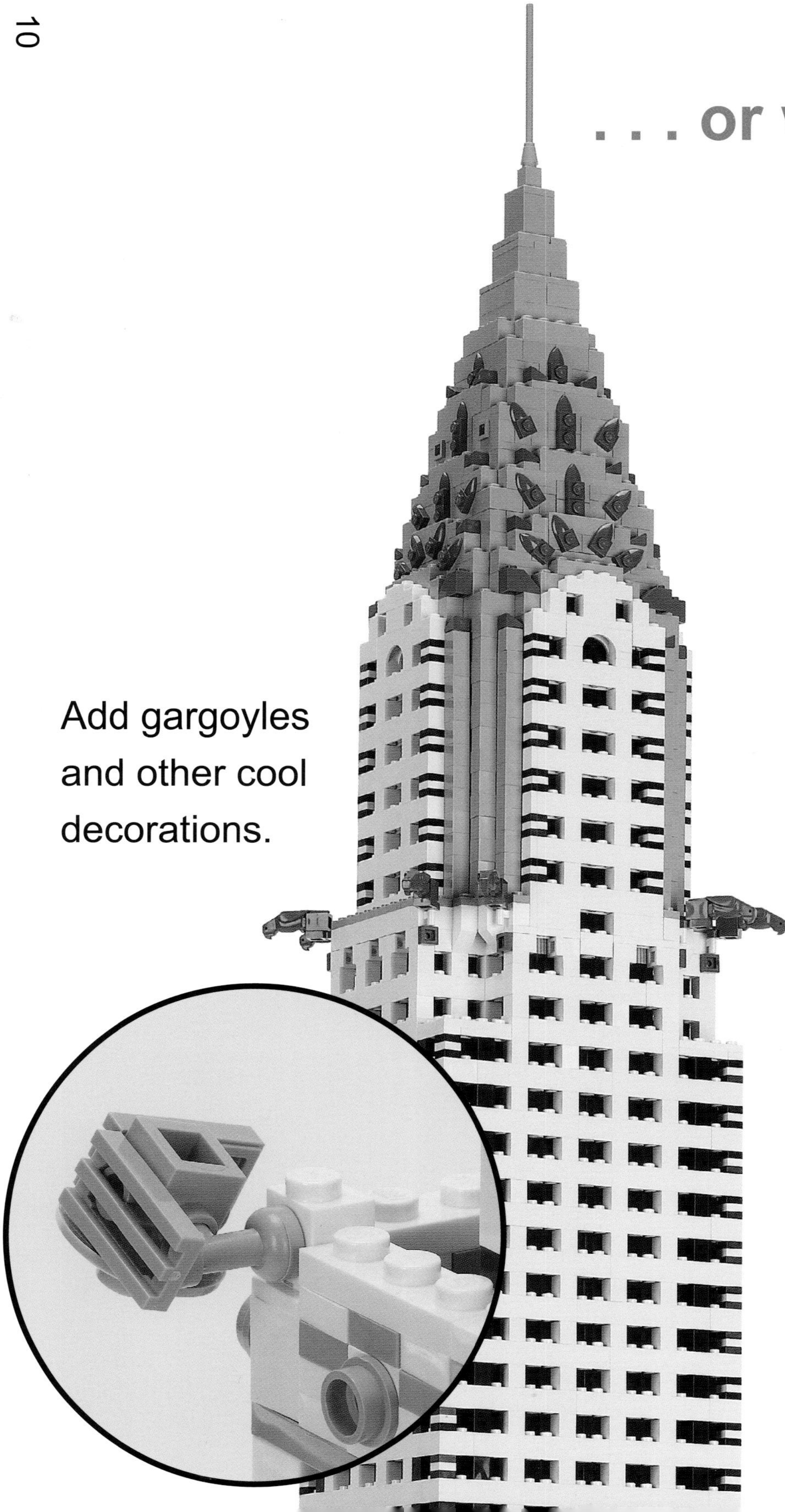

Your building will look even taller if you build the upper floors extra short.

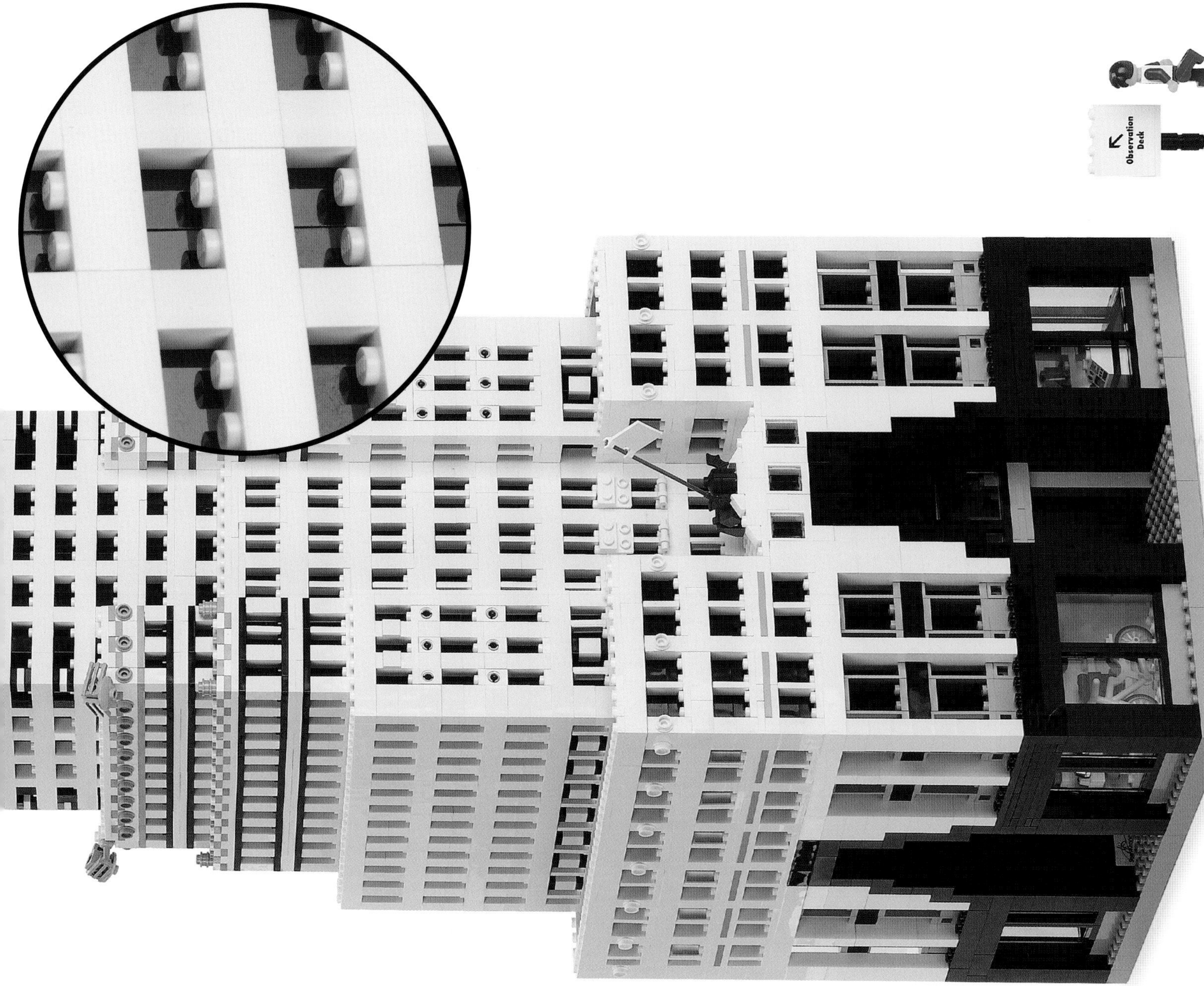
Observation Deck

What a great view of the city!

Make a mini metropolis.

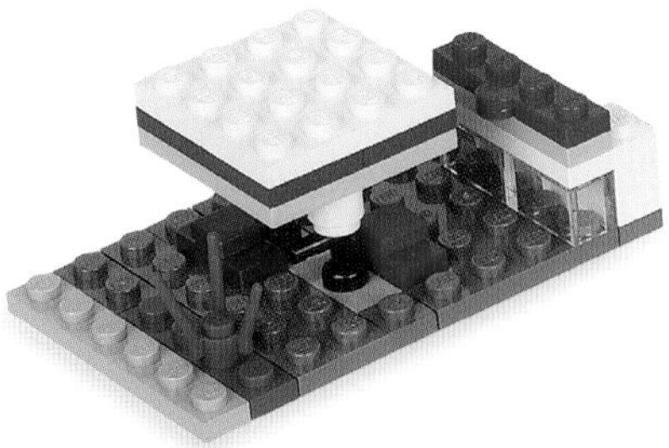

Gas station

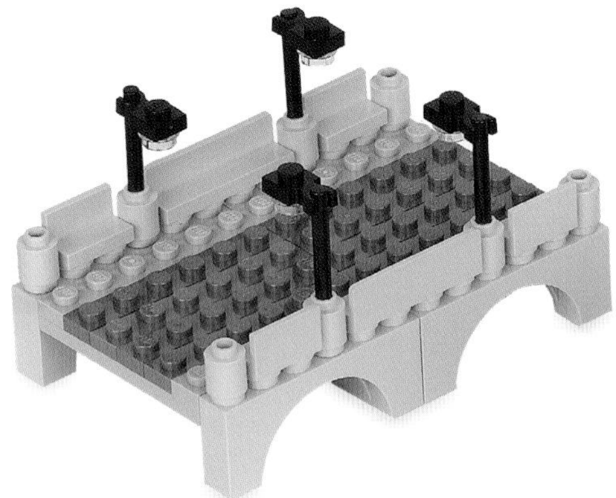

Bridge

Firehouse

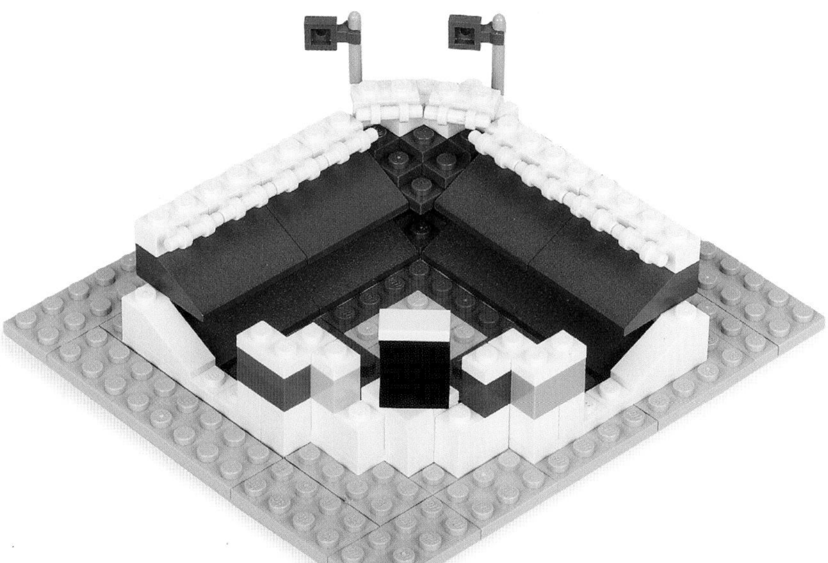

Stadium

Shipyard

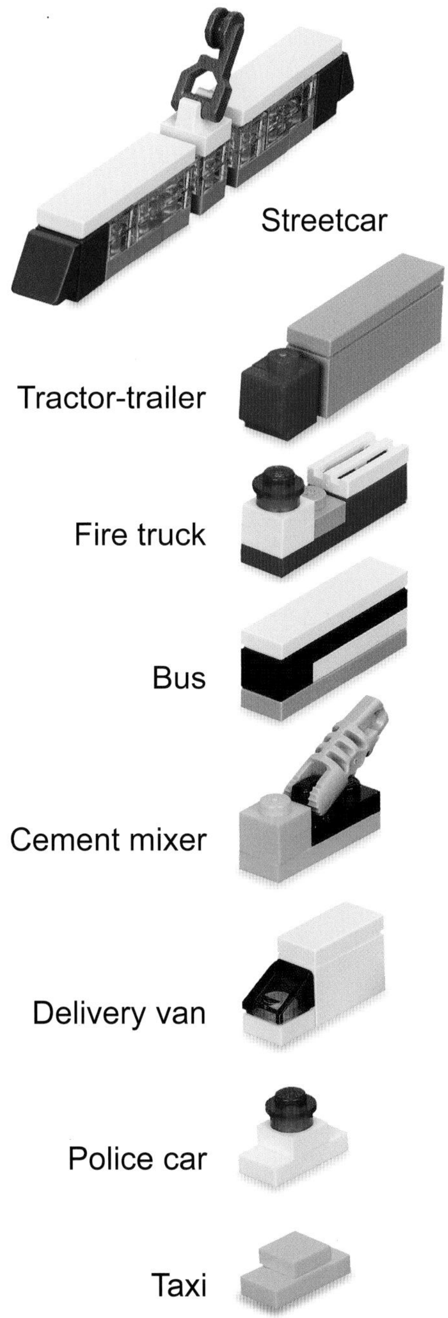
Streetcar
Tractor-trailer
Fire truck
Bus
Cement mixer
Delivery van
Police car
Taxi

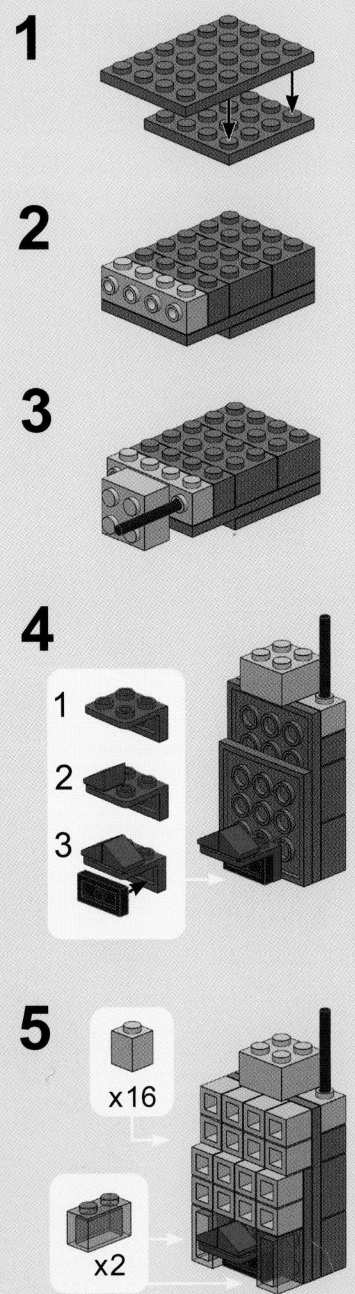
1
2
3
4
1
2
3
5
x16
x2

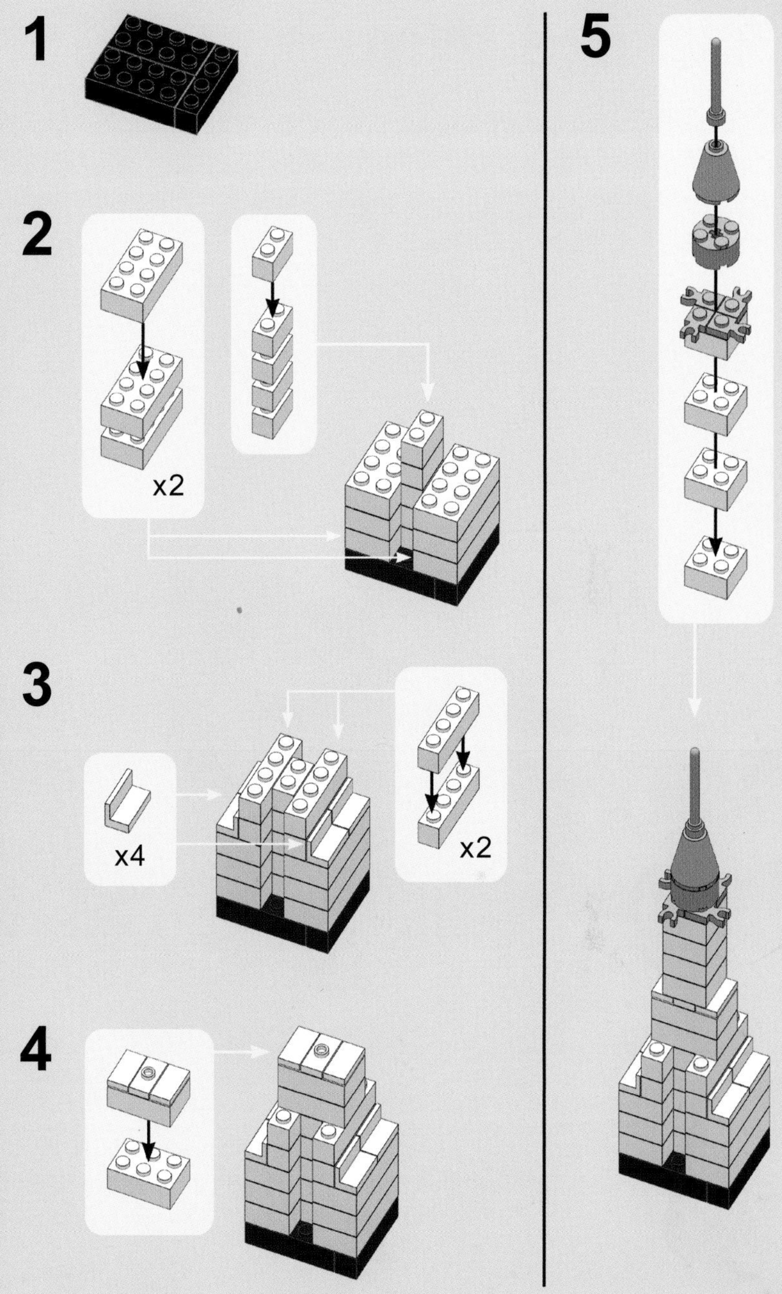
1
2
x2
3
x4
x2
4
5

Oh no! Who will fix the traffic jam?

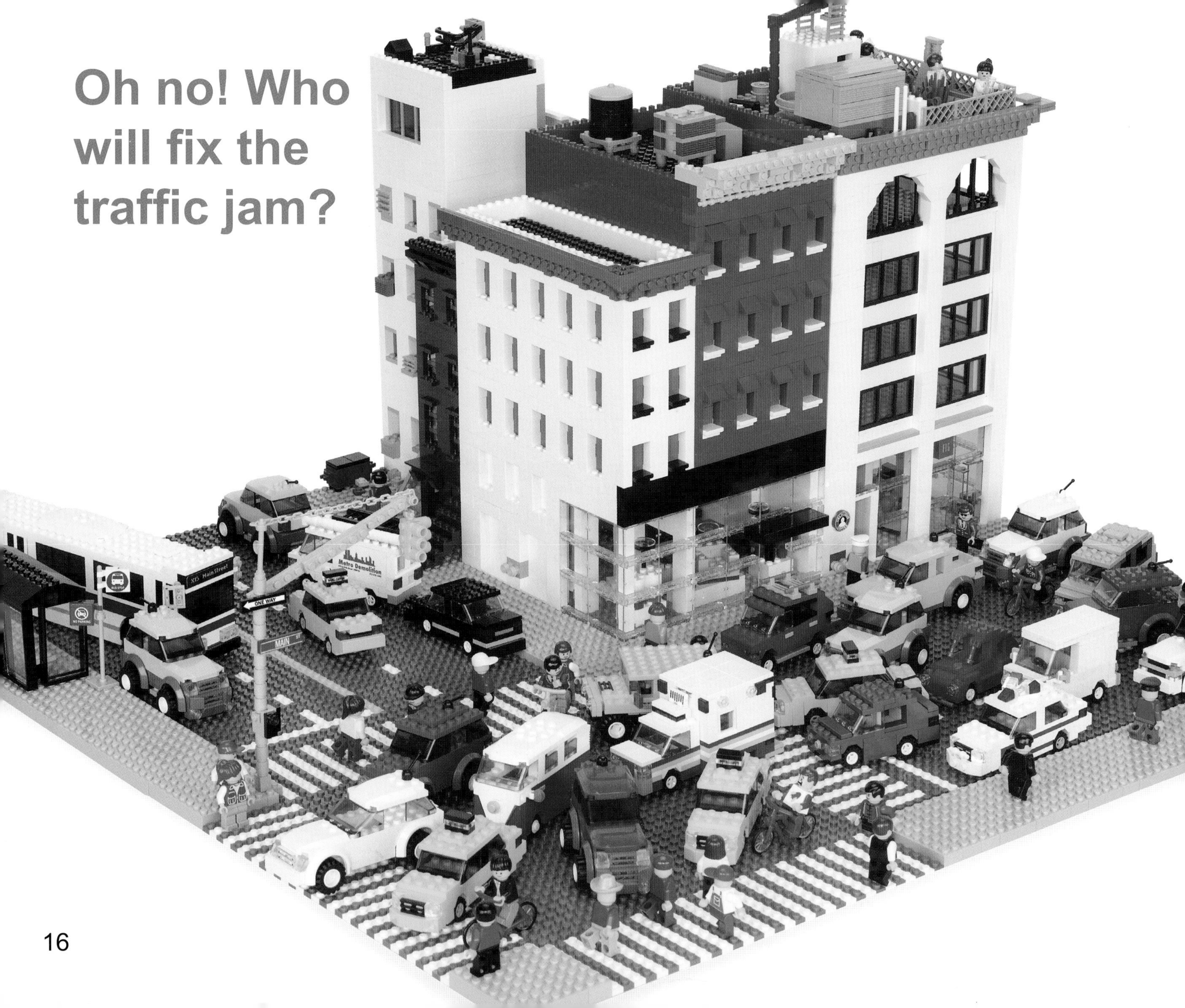

All clear!

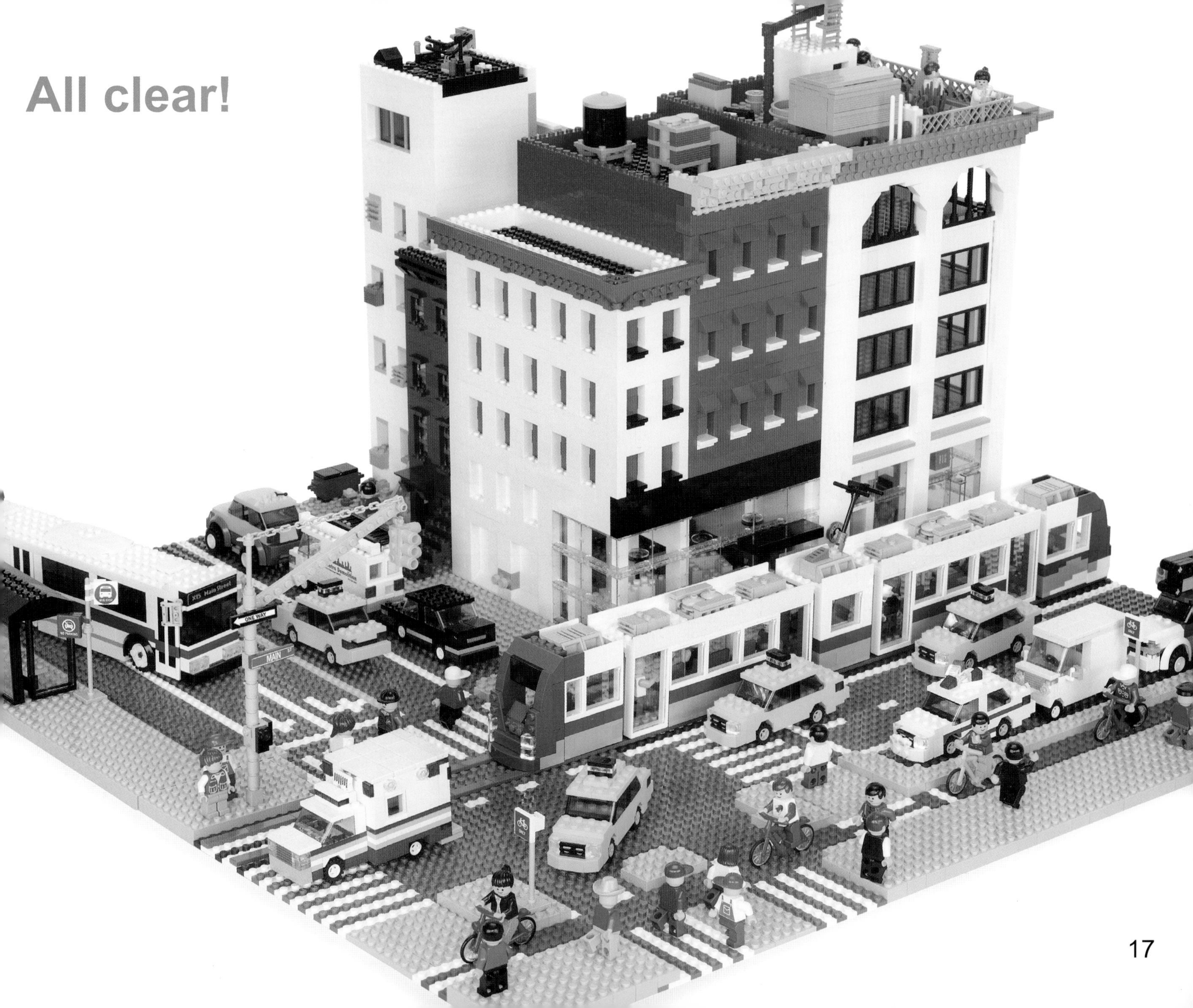

Give your street some furniture.

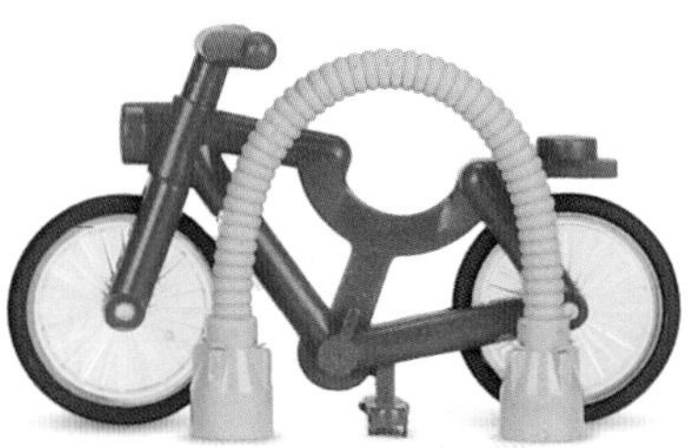

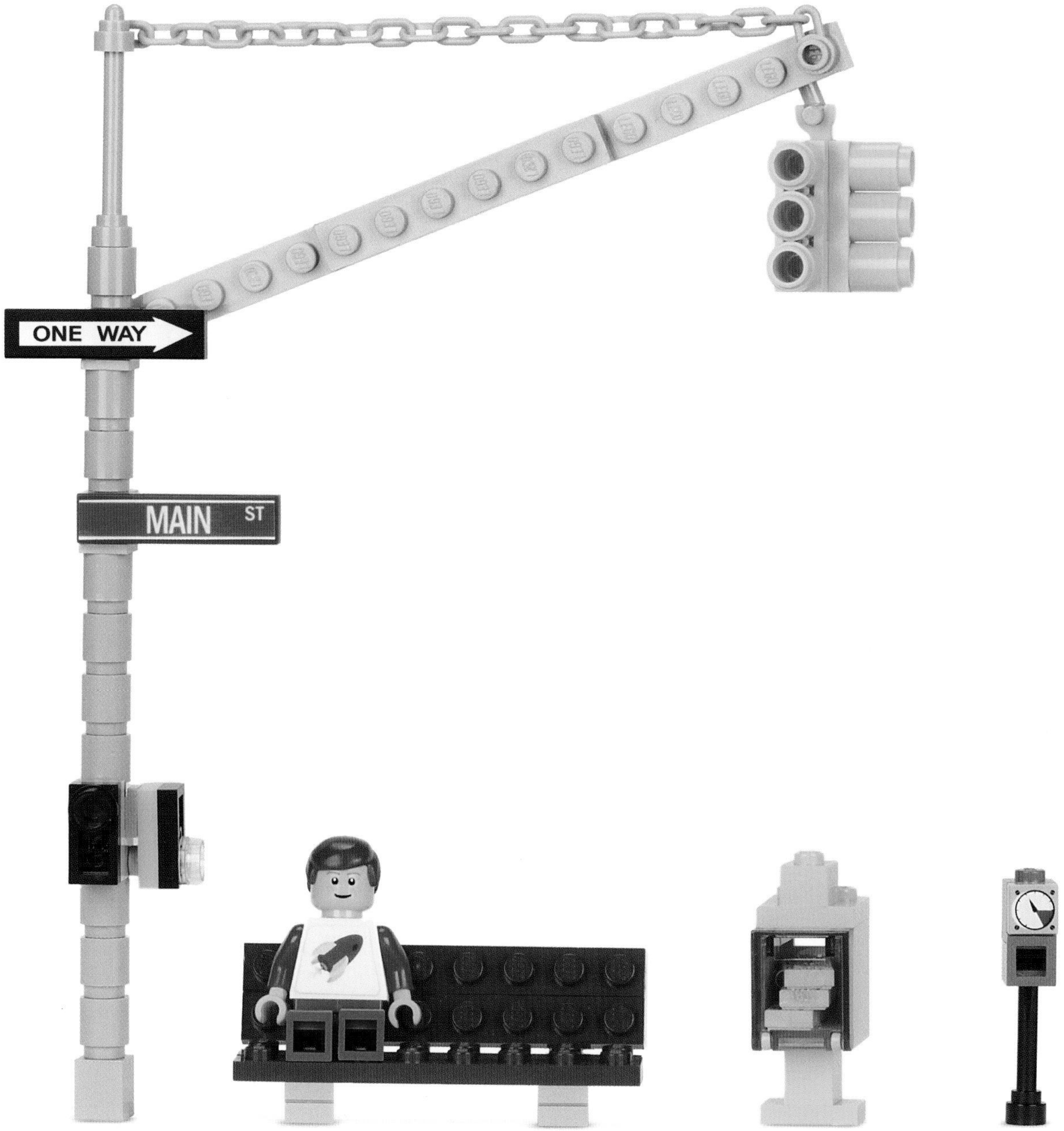
ONE WAY
MAIN ST

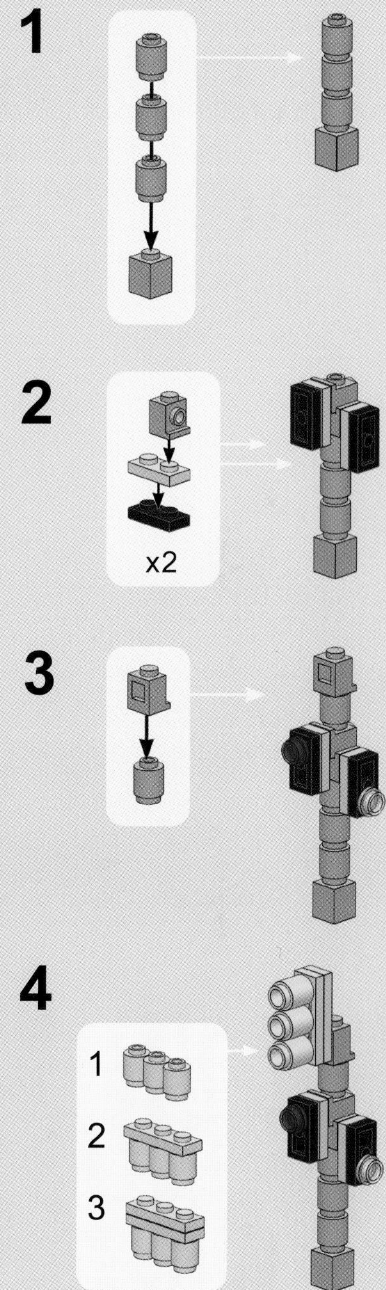
1
2
x2
3
4
1
2
3

Different building styles make the city interesting.

New building

Old building

Big building

Small building

Build some buildings

Make your own designs with whatever pieces you have.

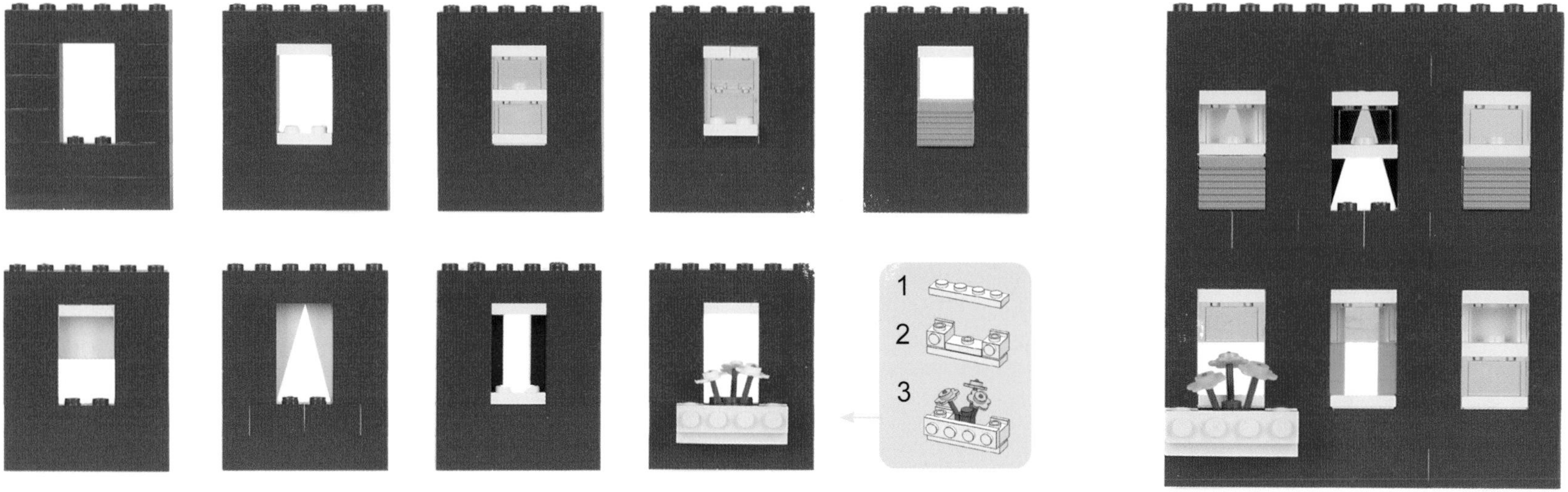

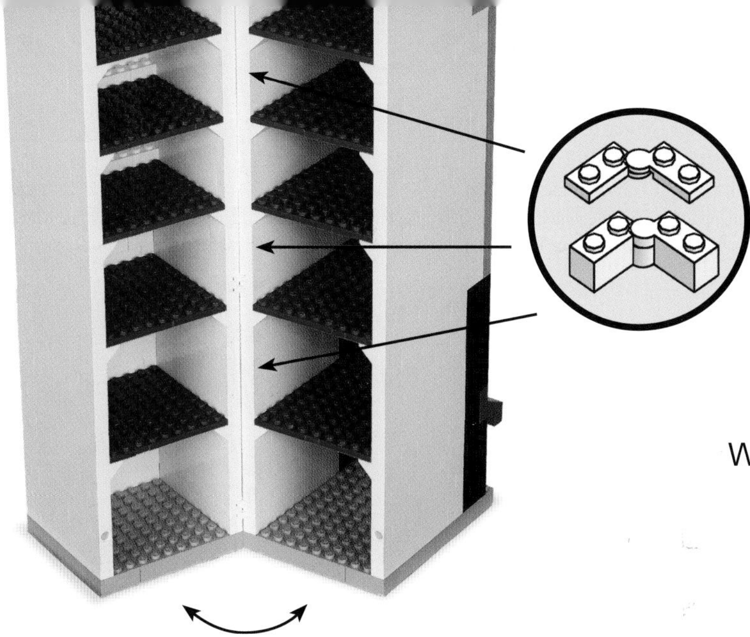

Open the hinges to play inside!

Use your extra colors on walls you won't see.

Buildings have lots of cool "roof junk."

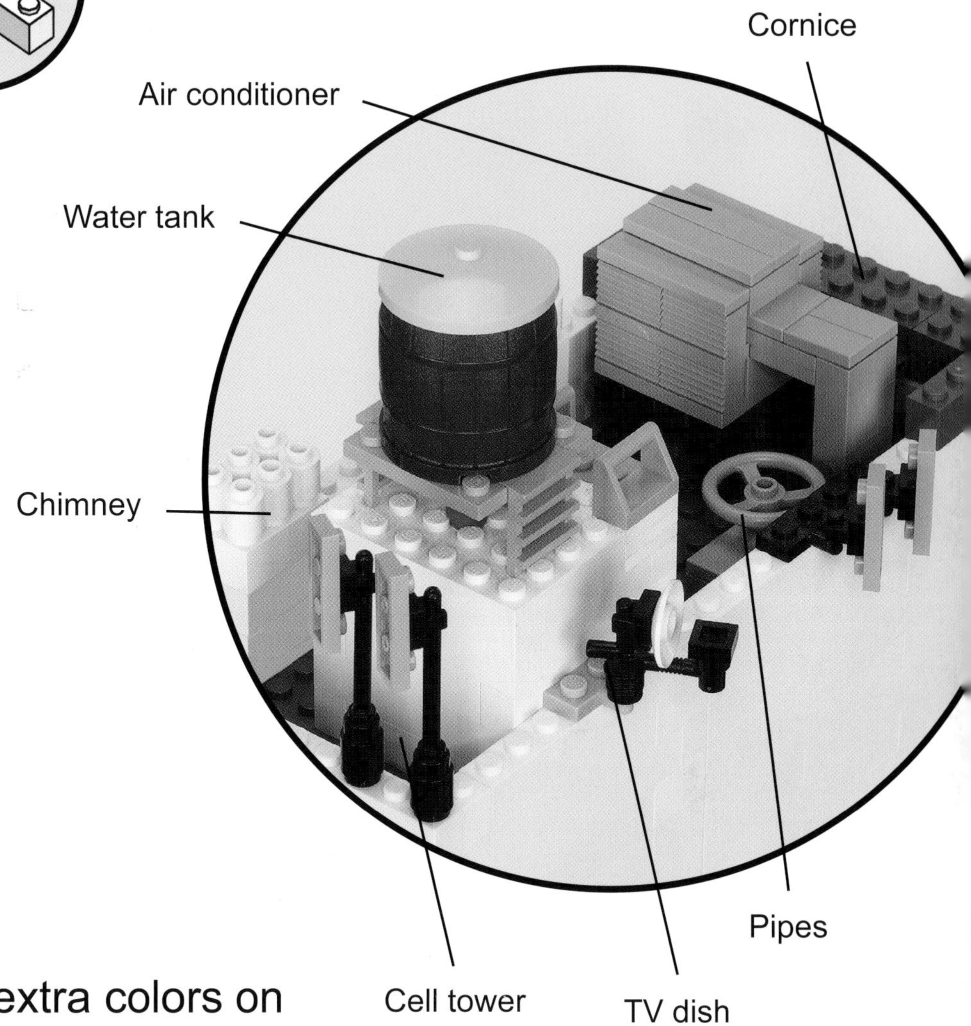

Make a home on Main Street.

1

2

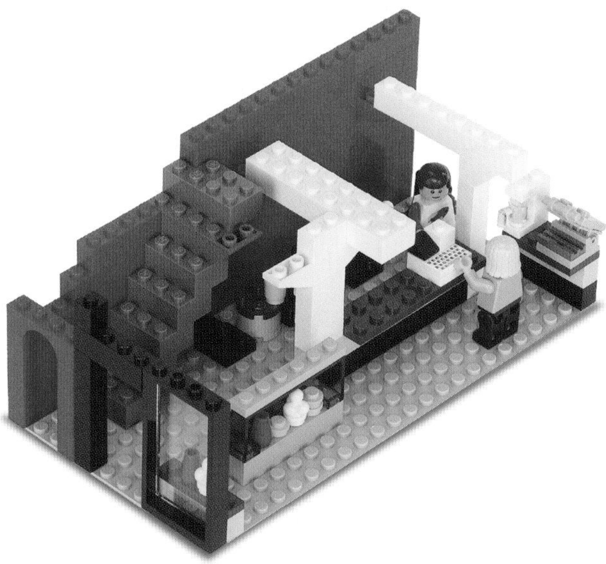

3

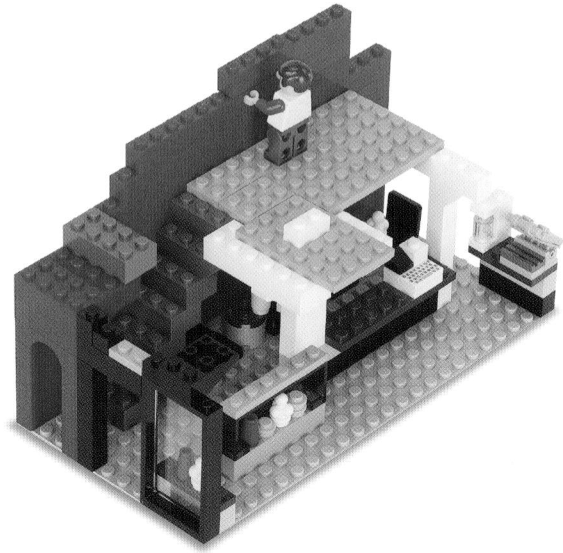

4

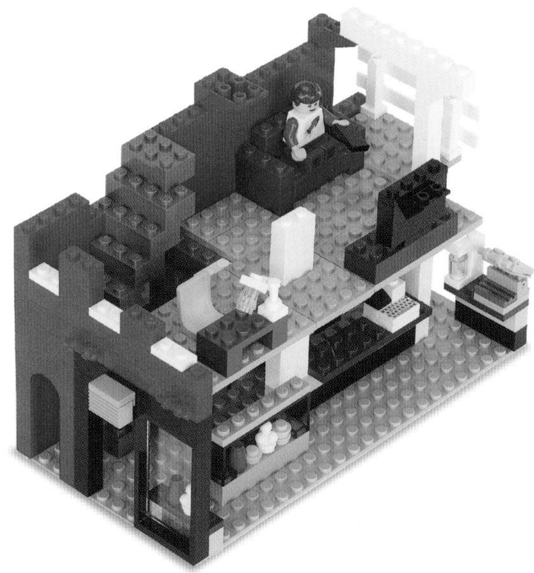

5

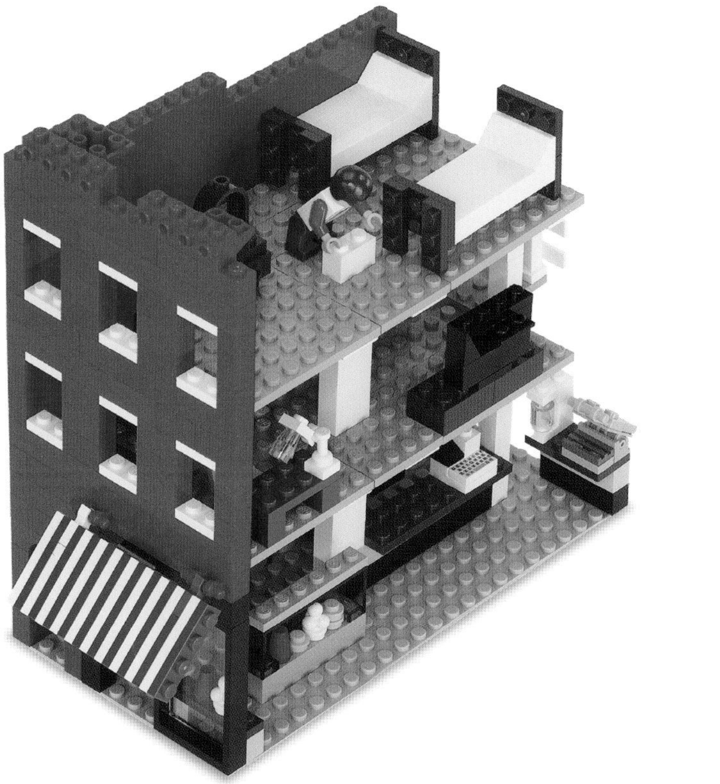

6

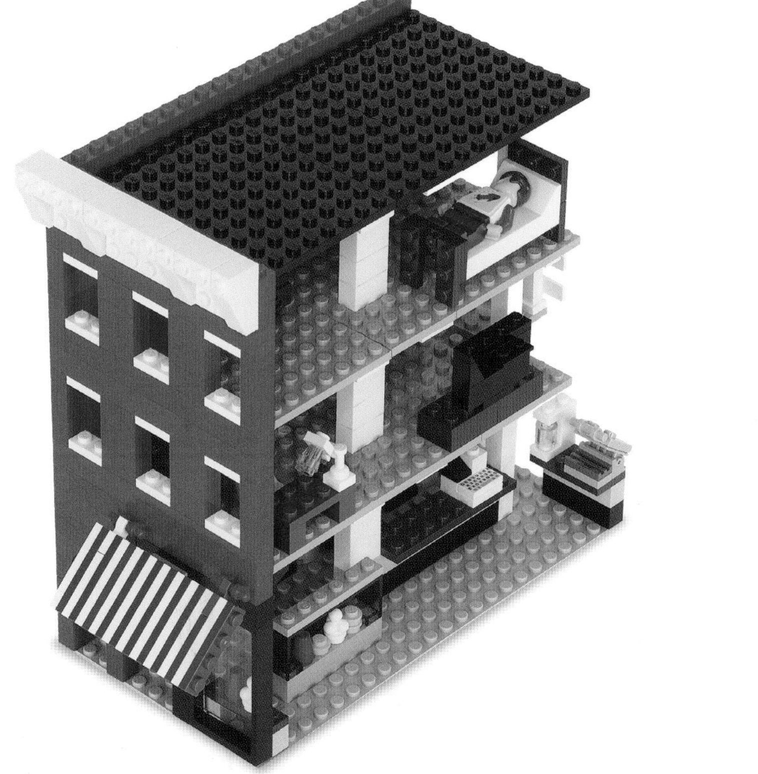

Ride the elevator and visit a home in the sky!

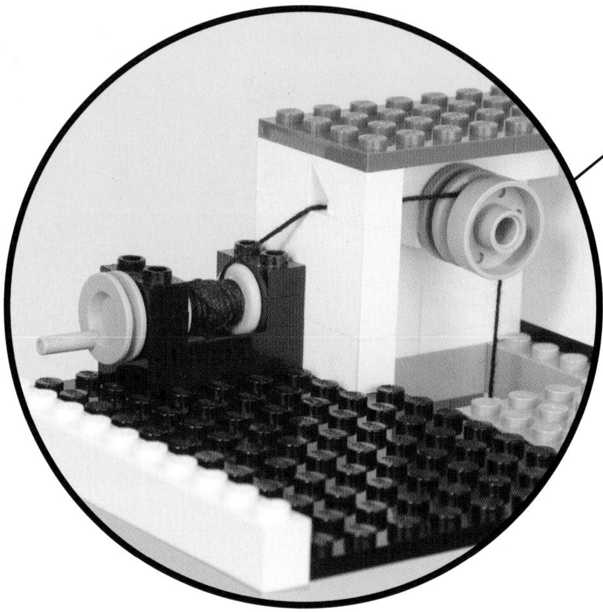

Use a pulley to make your elevator actually work.

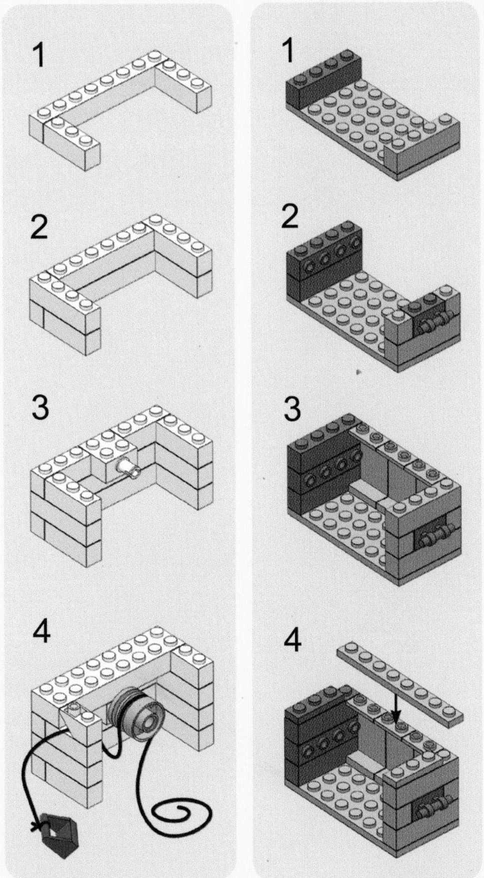

1

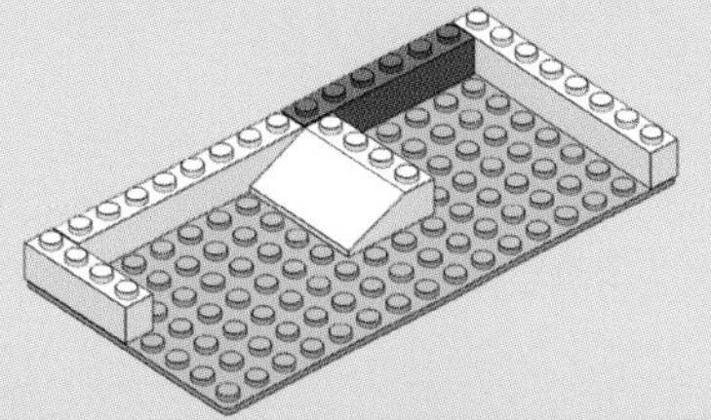

2

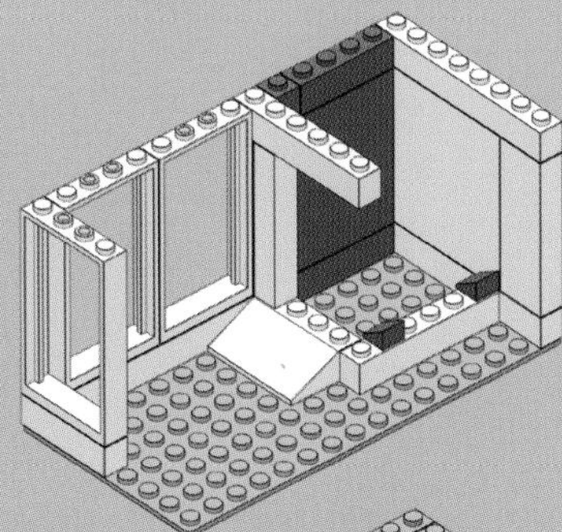

3

4

x 4
floors

5

More than just buildings

Things to do and places to go make the city exciting!

1

2

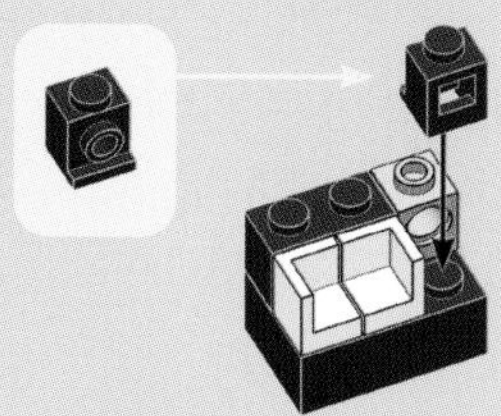

3

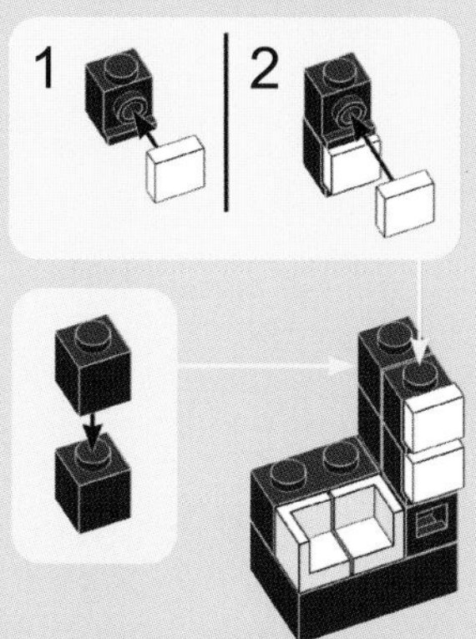

4

5

1

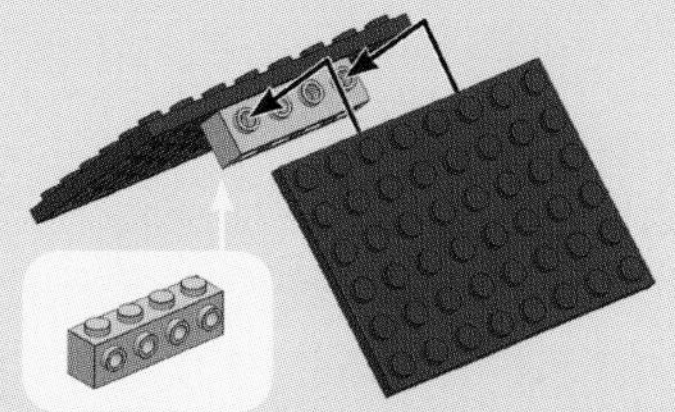

2

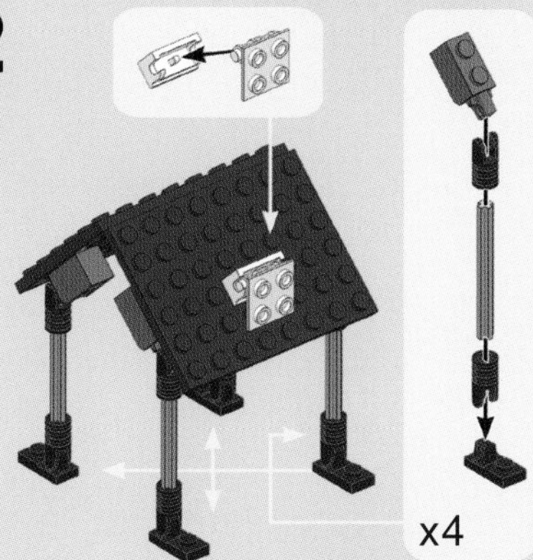

3

4

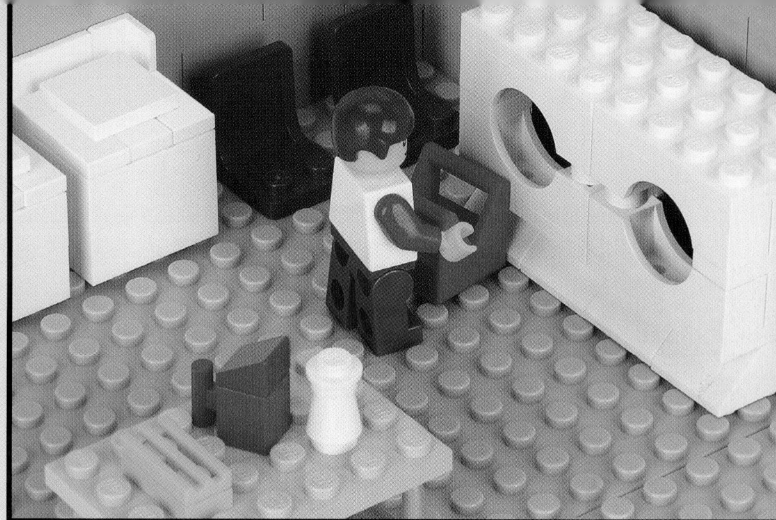

What else can you add to your city to bring it to life?

About Sean

Sean Kenney is a LEGO Certified Professional who has been building cities with LEGO bricks for over 30 years. He builds all day at his studio in New York City and likes to prove you can make anything with LEGO bricks.

Sean, at age 11, and his city

Visit Sean at www.seankenney.com to:

- Share your cool city creations with kids around the world
- Order some extra LEGO pieces
- See more cool city creations
- Find out if Sean is coming to your neighborhood . . . and more.

Cool City Stickers

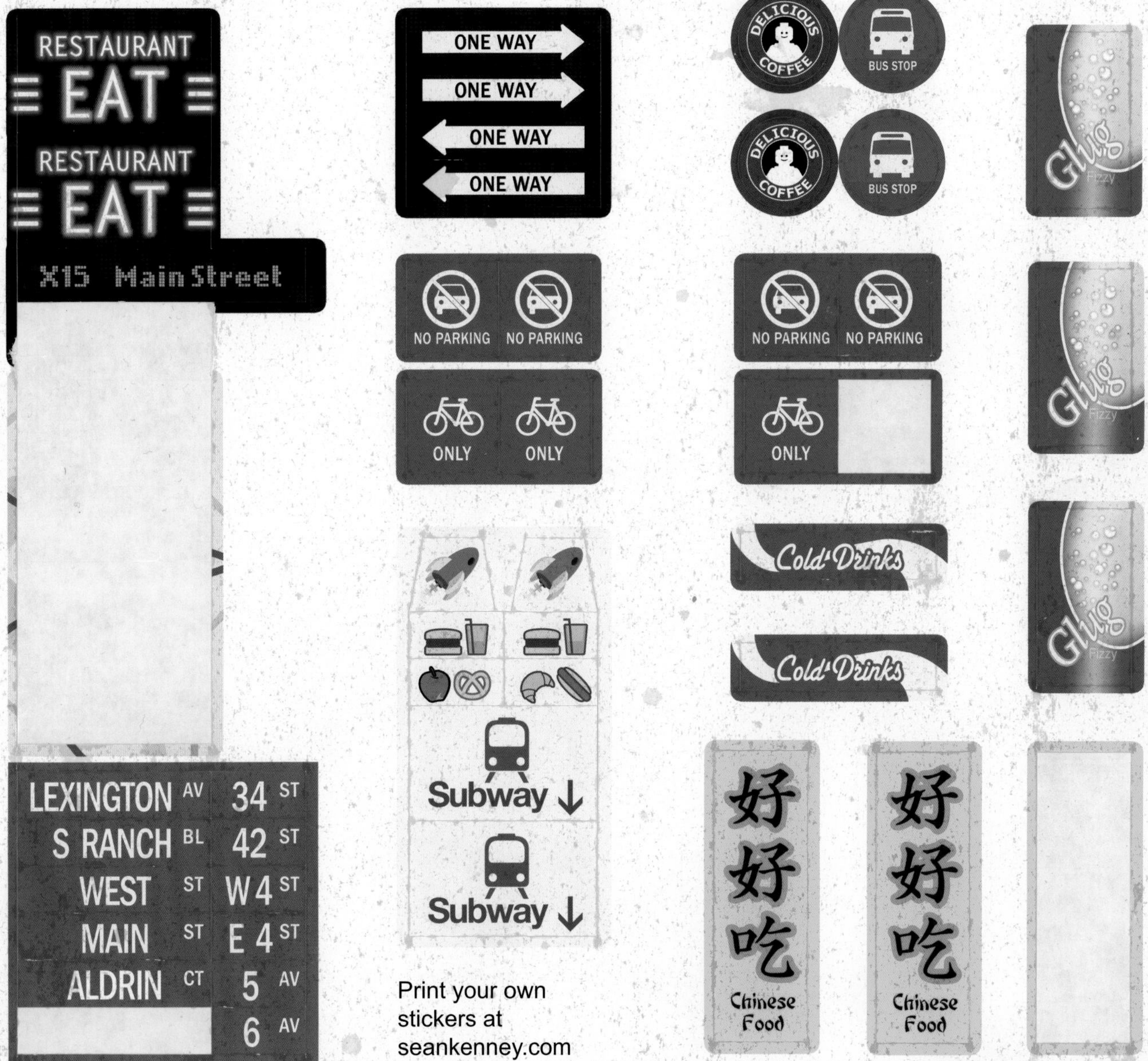

Print your own stickers at seankenney.com

Christy Ottaviano Books